Fish

Christine Butterworth and Donna Bailey

Silver Burdett Press, Morristown, New Jersey

These are my pet goldfish.
I call them Goldie, Buster,
Wavy, and Fred.

2

Goldie is red and gold.

She has a small tail. She has small fins.

Buster has a big tail.

He has big fins, too.

He swims very fast.

Wavy has a long tail.
It waves when she swims.

Fred is a black goldfish.

Have you ever seen a fish like Fred?

Fred has a wavy tail.

He has big round eyes.

They help him to see all around.

I feed my goldfish every day.
I drop their food onto the water.

8

The food sinks in the water.
The fish can eat it now.

Fish open and close their mouths
as they swim.
This is how they get air
from the water.

The water goes into their mouths.
Can you see their gills?
They are at the back of their heads.
The water comes out of their gills.

My tank has an air pump.
The air pump puts air
in the water for the fish.

Goldfish are freshwater fish.

Freshwater fish live in ponds and rivers.

14

There are stones in my tank. They are like the stones at the bottom of a river.

I have some plants in my tank.
I have snails, too.

The snails eat the green slime.

The plants keep the water fresh.

Goldfish like to swim in clean water.

Look at the different fish
in this big tank.
They are all freshwater fish.
Can you see the plants?
Can you see the air bubbles?

Some people keep saltwater fish.
Saltwater fish live in the sea.

Many pretty saltwater fish live
near coral reefs.

These fish live near coral reefs.
They are clown fish.

This is a parrot fish.

It scrapes its food off the coral.

It uses its nose.

These are golden butterfly fish.

Look at their long noses.

What do you think

their noses are for?

A butterfly fish pushes its long nose
into holes in the coral.
This is the way it finds food.

This puffer fish lives
near coral reefs, too.
Puffer fish cannot swim very fast.

24

When a puffer fish is afraid, it puffs up.
Then it looks big and brave.

This is a stone fish.

It looks like the coral.

It stings other fish and kills them.

This ugly fish is a blenny.
It can change its color
and hide in the coral.

Some blenny are very smart.

They can leave the water.

They can find food
on the rocks.

This strange fish is a seahorse.

It stands on its tail when it swims.

The female seahorse lays her eggs.
She lays them in a pouch.
It is on the male's belly.

30

The eggs hatch. The baby seahorses
come out of the pouch. They swim away.

There are many strange fish in the world.
People like to keep pretty fish as pets
These pretty fish are angel fish.

Reading consultant: Diana Bentley
Editorial consultant: Donna Bailey

Illustrated by Gill Tomblin
Picture research by Suzanne Williams
Designed by Richard Garratt Design

First published in 1988 by
Macmillan Children's Books,
a division of Macmillan Publishers Limited
4 Little Essex Street, London WC2R 3LF and Basingstoke

Published in the United States by
Silver Burdett Press, Morristown, New Jersey.

Printed in Hong Kong

Library of Congress Cataloging-in-Publication Data
Butterworth, Christine.
    Fish.
    (My world——red series)
    Summary: A child discusses the care, feeding, and
activities of four pet goldfish. Also describes the
characteristics of other types of fish, including the
parrot fish, puffer fish, and blenny.
    1. Fishes——Juvenile literature.   [1. Fishes]
I. Tomblin, Gill, ill.   II. Title.   III. Series:
Butterworth, Christine.   My world——red series.
QL617.2.B88 1988   597   87-23395
ISBN 0-382-09546-4

All photographs by Peter Greenland except:
Cover: ZEFA (C. Voigt)
Bruce Coleman: 20 (C. B. Frith), 23 (Jon Kenfield), 28 & 29
    (Jane Burton)
Oxford Scientific Films: 24 & 25 (David Thompson)
Planet Earth/Seaphot: 21 (Hugh Jones), 22, 27 & 32 (Peter
    Scoones)
ZEFA: 17 (Corneel Voigt), 26 W. Schmidt)